# Bridgewatcher
## & *Other Poems*

London

**SPM Publications**
Unit 136, 113-115 George Lane, South Woodford,
London E18 1AB, United Kingdom
www.spmpublications.com

First published in Great Britain by SPM Publications – an imprint of Sentinel Writing & Publishing Company Limited in association with Eastern Light EPM Ltd (organisers of the Excel for Charity International Writing Competition Series) in December 2013.

Copyright ©2013 The Authors

The contributors named in this book have asserted their moral rights under the Copyright, Designs and Patents Act 1988, to be identified as the editors and authors of this work.

ISBN 978-0-9927055-5-8

All rights reserved. No part of this publication may be reproduced, stored in or introduced into a retrieval system, or transmitted, in any form, or by any means (electronic, mechanical, photocopying, scanning, recording or otherwise) without the prior written permission of both the above-named copyright owner and the publisher.

Book design by Nnorom Azuonye

Set in Palatino

# Bridgewatcher
# & *Other Poems*

Edited by
## Mandy Pannett

## Other titles from SPM Publications

### Anthologies
- *Sentinel Annual Literature Anthology* (2011. Editors: Nnorom Azuonye, Unoma Azuah, Amanda Sington-Williams)

### Short Fiction
- *First Flame* by Bruce Harris (2013.)

### Poetry
- *The Bridge Selection* by Nnorom Azuonye (2012)
- *Marking Time* by Roger Elkin (2012)
- *All the Invisibles* by Mandy Pannett (2012)
- *Letter Home & Biafran Nights* by Afam Akeh (2012)
- *Nine East* by Uche Nduka (2013)
- *Triptych* by Obemata (2013)

### Drama
- *The Candles* by Uche-Chinemere Nwaozuzu (2012)

These books are available directly from
www.spmpublications.com
and from all Amazon channels, Barnes & Noble and other bookstores.

### Poetry Books by Mandy Pannett

- *All the Invisibles*
- *Allotments in the Orbital*
- *Bee Purple*
- *Frost Hollow*

# Contents

Foreword   9

The Psychiatry Research Trust Poetry Competition (2013)
An Adjudication Report by Mandy Pannett   10

**NICK PEMBERTON**
Message to My Son   13
Poem for a Younger Wife   14
Picture Book   16
Sorting the Empties   18

**DANIEL ROY CONNELLY**
Simon Magus   19

**PENNY SHUTT**
Bridgewatcher   20
Pseudoseizures   22

**DESMOND KON ZHICHENG-MINGDÉ**
The Old Schoolyard   24
Reading Trakl and Wittgenstein in a Barnako Prison   26

**KATELIN FARNSWORTH**
Faceless flowers   30

**MARGARET WILMOT**
Bonfire Ashes   32

**REHAN QAYOOM**
Africa Come Back   34

**SHEILA HAMILTON**
Antscape, Hungary   36

**PAT BORTHWICK**
Vanishing Trick   37

**BRIGID MURRAY**
Seeing the Sun   38
Hand-Foot Coordinates   39

**KATE HARMOND ALLAN**
Beginning   40

**MIRIAM PATRICK**
Dwelling Place   41

**PAT BOWEN**
Kelp Stalk   42
Taking the Weight   43

**CHRISTOPHER LUCK**
Till the puffling comes   44

**ALEX HAMILTON-BROWN**
The Garden   46

**CHARLOTTE GANN**
Gordon's   48

**E.E. NOBBS**
Altitudes of Meeting and Parting   49

**DENISE MCSHEEHY**
Flood   50
Addicted   51

**OZ HARDWICK**
Saturday Blues   52
The Gift   54
The Mandolin Lesson   55

**ROGER ELKIN**
Patchwork Language   56

**GABRIEL GRIFFIN**
Web Weaver   58

**MARK TOTTERDELL**
Niche   59

**VALERIE BRIDGE**
I remember leaving   60

**CAMILLA LAMBERT**
Acting My Age   62
Frou-frou at the Panorama   64

**CHRIS MCLAUGHLIN**
Perspective   65

**TONY WATTS**
Five poets take a walk in the country   66

**ROBIN LINDSAY WILSON**
The Cure   69

**LYDIA SUAREZ**
The Green Post   70

**JENNY DONNISON**
Memento Mori   71

**ANNE HAMLETT**
Spinning Time    72
You should go ...    74

**MARY OLIVER**
The Exploding Horse, 1922    76

**A.C. CLARKE**
Girl in Bath Street    79
Wild Peter    80

**MARIA BENNETT**
Evening Came and Morning Came    82

**MANTZ YORKE**
Endurance    84

# Foreword

The poems in this anthology have been written by poets dancing in the best circles of their craft. In reading the feast of poetry presented here you will encounter fully matured hands in control of their craft. What is more, the poets in this collection are also very generous spirits.

These poems have been selected by poet Mandy Pannett from entries to the Psychiatry Research Trust Poetry Competition (2013). Mandy is an accomplished poet in her own right with four poetry collections of her own. She is also the Poetry Editor of Sentinel Literary Quarterly. Her judgment in the selection and editing of the poems in this anthology is highly commendable and admirable.

We hope that this book will do well for the charity. In addition to donations from the competition entries, we shall be donating 2.50 from every copy of this book sold to the Psychiatry Research Trust and information on all donations will be published in the Excel for Charity News Blog.

I am thankful to the poets who entered the competition, every one of the entrants – not just those who made the anthology. Without your support we would not have made it.

Incidentally following the conclusion of this competition we have been reimagining the Excel for Charity Competitions and hope to re-launch them in January 2015 with a focus on publishing anthologies of the best works and raising as much funds as possible for the charities.

Nnorom Azuonye
Administrator,
Excel for Charity International Writing Competitions.

# The Psychiatry Research Trust Poetry Competition (2013)
## An Adjudication Report

# Mandy Pannett

There was a very strong selection of poems entered for this competition. Maybe an underlying awareness of the chosen charity contributed to the number of poems that came over as both personal and reflective – an overwhelming number touched on the theme of memory, its importance and strengths as well as its transience and loss.

I had no problem choosing my winners. The problems came with the ones I had to leave out. There were many that couldn't make the final list and I can't list them all here. I must mention one in particular – 'The Green Post'. I was sad not to be able to place such an excellent poem.

A quick mention also for the following: 'Flood', 'Dwelling Place', 'Beginning', 'Kelp Stalk', 'Vanishing Trick'. All these, together with the winning poems and many other strong contenders will, I hope, be in this autumn's anthology where others may share my enjoyment.

### 1ST Bridgewatcher by Penny Shutt

I have read this piece countless times now and each time it strikes me as faultless, a perfect poem. The reader is led slowly through the situation – a patient who toys with the 'quivering possibility' of suicide' and a psychiatrist/doctor who, while feeling powerless to help except with medication, can empathise with the horror of the childhood experience of seeing a man 'let go and drop' from a bridge into the 'unshimmering depths'. The memory of this shocking event includes not only the actual falling but the heart stopping seconds before, the 'sickening courage/of that hand/letting go of the rail.'

'Bridgewatcher' is an unforgettable poem, well-crafted and written with sensitivity and compassion. An outstanding winner.

## 2nd Pseudoseizures by Penny Shutt

This poem is both beautiful and shocking – beautiful in the way it describes the 'comfort' in defencelessness of a seizure and shocking in the relentless detailing of the stages of convulsion and the poignancy of the years of endurance since the 'original undoing' of the 'nine year old self'.

There is so much to admire in this brave and important poem, particularly the poet's careful and delicate use of language to peel back the layers of an experience in which the seizure itself feels almost orgasmic in its reaching the 'very crux' of 'self-abandonment'.

## 3rd The Old School yard by Desmond Kon Zhicheng-Mingde

This is a poem about the sadness and pain of nostalgia with its overlay of loss and impermanence.

I have particularly selected this poem as a winner for its choice of evocative details, the careful delineation of the four friends and the need they share for dreams and imagined lives and also for the bitter-sweet poignancy of the 'litany' of experiences which may be seen as no more than 'postcards' or 'scrawled prattle' but which, somewhere in the depths of memory, are still 'precious'.

**Highly Commended: picture book by Nick Pemberton**

It was a joy to find this poem among the entries – the kind of writing I love that explores and imaginatively plays with language. The repetitions of phrases and images are used so skilfully here, revealing layers and layers of meaning through the subtleties of words.

**Highly Commended: Faceless flowers by Katelin Farnsworth**

Here we have an almost unbearably sad poem which I chose for its structure, its back story, its careful selection of details to convey emotions and for such perfect lines as 'feelings rubbing, battling the days, the sun streaming in, the sky cracking, my words falling like silk.'
A beautiful poem. I wish it could have been placed higher.

My congratulations to the winners and many thanks to all entrants.

Mandy Pannett

# MESSAGE TO MY SON

## Nick Pemberton

Where is your pen? Where are your shoes?
Or your passport? Or the money for your lunch?
Or the note that says you have lost these things
But should be humoured? It seems sometimes that
Your forgetfulness is a search for an escape from things
You find tedious and, in choosing this path, you have
Discovered a tunnel that leads back to a deep lost continent
Of dreams, where lion and lamb, weary of waiting for the day
They will lie down together have decided instead
To make common cause with the dolphins.

I remember seventeen years since
On a surf rumbling Pembrokeshire beach
Beneath a tumbling cathedral of clouds
Remade as streaming pennants in the wind
You sat for hours while the sun burned your back
And your eyes traced the shape of a seashell
Held in your hand. Because you choose to lose yourself
In such wonder, I do more than humour your quiet humour,
I honour it. Still, as parent, for some years yet,
I am honour bound to ask: this road you have chosen
Like the elegant spiral of the shell that leads from its
Sculpted frozen lip inward, back through ever tighter coiled
Time to the moment that saw it first created,
Where does it end? And if we ever get there
Do you think we'll need shoes?

Amongst the world's seductive whispers let me say:
It takes a kind of forthright guile
to answer complex questions with a smile.

## POEM FOR A YOUNGER WIFE

### Nick Pemberton

Together we skirt the perimeters
of our shared ecology. Birds migrate
southward and leave heartbeats in her blue breast.
She feels sun in the structures and hollows

of her bones. The porous rainclouds are wet
on her lip as she bites. We live, she and I
(her and me), in a town where rules are soon
to be suspended. We read the signs we need.

In the kids' pictures tacked to the fridge
stands a painted, nameless, numberless house
with gate, fence and path, tree, stream and bridge
 -a place where beasts are transformed by her love.

I would solve her riddles,
return favours for her if I could,
seek amongst strangers a saviour
mild and implacable as the rise and fall of the tide
to cherish and nurture her when I am dead.

Folk fall out. They fall out of her sky.
She populates the land between us
with quirks and whispers. The dark of her eye
reflects back asymmetric palindromes
chased into the burnished weave of waves that break
on the world's frayed, unravelling hem.

Love, lose, solve, evolve.

We burrow blindly to this edge alone
but turn back together: -from the icy wheel of stars
to the ache of weather & light, the steel
in the blade of grass, and the mark of a sleek
cubs' pawprints on the cold, white door.

# PICTURE BOOK

## Nick Pemberton

Here's a book, a picture book,
a picture book that shows to us
a single moment in a day, frozen fast in a book that says:

here's a book, a picture book,
stuffed with dreams and love and stuff,
a picture book that shows to us
men and women who've had enough
of a single moment in a day, frozen fast in a book that says
that -for this moment- there is only this:

-just this book, this picture book,
just one more book, like other books all
stuffed with dreams and love and stuff,
so take it down and take a close hard look.
This picture book will show to us
-torn jacket, cracked spine, its jacket scuffed-
men and women who've had enough
and grown weary of picturing a picture of a picture
of a single moment in a day, frozen fast in a book that says
*(like water on a pebble that the sunlight will erase)*
that in this life there's only this:
the imprint of a lover's kiss.

Here's a book, a picture book,
a magic book, although it looks
just one more book, like other books all
slumped in ragged rows on shelves
stuffed with dreams and love.... and stuff
that skips like the moon on the water between us.
So take it down and take a close hard look

and listen too, to all that moves within this book.
This picture book will speak to us
-torn jacket, cracked spine, its jacket scuffed-
and take us to another place, a shared time full
of men and women who've had enough
wit and sense not to simply dream of dreaming
or picturing a picture of a picture of a picture.
They are true dreamers.  They dream the present, not the past,
not just a single moment in a day, frozen fast in a book that says
that this moment is all there is. Instead,
they work and hope and wish
that -*like water on a pebble*- the sunlight will erase
the stain that spreads through all our days,
for in this life there's only this:
Every day's slow falling, slow falling away,
like snow falling softly as
the imprint of a lover's kiss.
The book is closed.  It was not much.
The book is closed.  The pages touch.

## SORTING THE EMPTIES

**Nick Pemberton**

Pets, parents, children, friends
go the same way as strangers
in the end. Mice, men, the best
laid plans all die. Don't cry.
Keep busy and give thanks.

When the tale that hooks each heartbeat
to the last starts to unwind
in the haywire scribble and bleep
of monitors, when we rise up
and wander the maze of hospital
corridors, looking for the door
that let us in and find instead
god only knows what... come near.
Help us join dot to last dot.
Whisper the words we need to hear.

And when we're gone, like I am gone,
ashes scattered, chatter chatted
amongst kindness, canapes and wreaths,
brush the dust from your shoe and go. Leave us
to blow and leach amongst beech trees, roots and rain
and know these words are true: *I love you.*

Okay. It's said. Now, since you're still here
go sort things out. The spirits were clear.
The wine was green. Brown was the beer.
It did not kill you, all the drink you drank.
You are not at peace. You are not content.
Instead you are happy. Give thanks.

# SIMON MAGUS

**Daniel Roy Connelly**

I remember one time
when Billie Collins read
in the tenth-century
church of Santa Francesca Romana
flanked by the martyrdom of St Lawrence
(Pietro da Cortona, 1646) and the spot
where the sorcerer Simon Magus died.

We had several opportunities to speak
at the reception that followed and when I left
Billie backed away from me to say quite simply
*You talked my fucking ear off all night long*
but which I still found quite poetic
and not lacking in a certain irony
given that his reading occupied
some of the night at least,
and then there's the painting
of a man being roasted alive
and the fact that the magician
who could levitate at will
fell down from the apse
and never flew again.

# BRIDGEWATCHER

**Penny Shutt**

I don't ask you to unbutton the sleeves
of your smart work shirt
to show me the cuts
because I believe you.

You tell me you typed 'suicide'
into *Google* again last night,
tell me about the website that came up
and I nod as though I don't know exactly
which one you mean.

I know it wasn't methods that work
you sought
but the solace of those voices
clamouring across the pages
for help amongst the helpless.

On the way into work, my train flies past
the bridge I know you go to.
In the morning glow, a crow perched on the railing,
it doesn't hold the same poignant splendour
I know it holds for you
at four a.m after the wine, the cider, the gin.

I know when you're up there
there's a certainty to the smooth flat concrete
below. That just grasping the cool steel
of the railing, toying
with that quivering possibility
is all the release that cutting
no longer gives.

I'm meant to be the one who manages this risk
but I don't
because I know that's not why you go there.
Instead, I up your antidepressants
so it looks like I did something.

As I write the prescription,
you recall a time when you were little,
the judder of the car across the Forth Road Bridge
the sparkle of South Queensferry
across the still black water
and the sudden horror
of seeing a man let go and drop
into the unglimmering depths,
flashing blue lights arriving seconds too late.

'Sometimes people just don't want to live anymore'
your dad tried to explain from the front
but he was driving, hadn't seen
what you had;
the sickening courage
of that hand
letting go of the rail.

# PSEUDOSEIZURES

**Penny Shutt**

And there's a seduction in returning
to those moments
in which we were most powerless.

There's a comfort
in seeing each writhing collapse
into self-abandonment
through to its completion,

to then tend to the mess
in the aftermath
of a drama you knew
you could have stopped

somewhere in the stillness
between myoclonus
and floor- juddering convulsions

If you had wanted to.

But you know you won't cease
until your limbs are spent
from each seizure's writhing throes,
your eyes roll expertly back, you stiffen-
then crumple
into the convulsion's familiar embrace
in the absence of an electrical discharge.

And you know you could just stop;
save yourself
the help you know you'll despise
in the post-ictal glare of day.

But something brings you back here
again,
and again
to the very crux of your defencelessness

to achieve nothing
but enduring separation
from the nine year old self
who endured
that original undoing.

# THE OLD SCHOOLYARD

## Desmond Kon Zhicheng-Mingdé

> *"Childhood is measured out by sounds and smells*
> *And sights, before the dark of reason grows."*
> ~ John Betjeman

We huddled under the lychgate, our names carved into its oak.
There was the smell of salt and fresh water, both in the air.

This was little shelter, barely keeping out the rain. Or comfort,
as Duncan brought up Browning, his poem about Porphyria.

Duncan saw himself as a tree. A Norway maple, limbs holding
up the sky. At North Petherwin, Hamish pointed to the snipe.

And how the squirrels here lived in shallow burrows,
instead of elms. Rupert once thought himself pregnant.

With river nymphs, those too gone with the light,
the light with every night, whether the day had been good.

Or less shiny than the one before. I was my own guilt
and evincement, tortured but graced. I was guileless, taciturn.

And unawares, walking in each of their shadows, as madcap
and feathered, walking into walls, our satchels left on the gravel.

And happily so, our dreams of imagined lives etched into bark.
Summers were long and reluctant. The tin miners. Assembly
line.

Drenched overalls, buckled heels. We were invisible, lunching
behind the backroom's generator. Leftovers wrapped for supper.

This year, the schoolyard looks more weathered than ever,
the scaffolding rising from the ground like a giant cage.

The chapel never had hidden rooms or a clock tower.
Or Porphyria. Its steeple now a bony maypole with limp flags.

The high fences that protected us, they now keep us out.
The dream of this life, its fuss and desire, as foreign a territory.

This life of corners, measured out in coffee breaks and a wall clock,
its analog numbers, interminable hours a tautening coil between.

Browning's Porphyria unmoved, undusted still-life on the wall.
She has the same wan expression, as forgotten an aphorism.

As her lover, as these strangers hunched over their workstations.
When will she stir, opal eyes, and wake to her indifference?

Feet off peddles, Duncan rode past the Douglas fir. No looking back.
His shadow following River Tamar, only to turn off at the bend.

The way the waters siphoned off into the smaller Inny.
Its strange litany of memories. Like postcards, scrawled prattle.

The four of us remembered one image clearly, without fiction.
Three sand martins hopping across rock and clay, to the road bridge.

A school of brown trout darting about. Just below us.
As if looking for something old and precious, more permanent.

# READING TRAKL AND WITTGENSTEIN IN A BARNAKO PRISON

## Desmond Kon Zhicheng-Mingdé

*"O God, what guilt and darkness we have to go through. O that we might not succumb in the end."*
~ Georg Trakl

In the barrel, a parting note rolled around a cigarette, smoke in filigree prints; each word ricocheting against another, truisms buried, filaments.

In echoes dulled but distinct, as if songs were meant to be played that way to the march of drums, cymbals, every metal, and angle of sound.

Against the alloy, initials engraving themselves, a soft felt, as faint a sign. Too worldly to capture, deep heaving, whole platoon of dying men.

Of darker months, tunnels like bolt carriers, black and channeling, cold steel to the touch, your books already in Galicia, in an abandoned alley.

Of the last pew, where you sat, fist in palm, shoulders trembling like a child's.
Of the unfamiliar and circuitous, of running home in midnight rain.

Alongside the structures - they did not exist, grey barracks an ephemeral arc.
Also a correspondence, trajectories, a sure-footed trek into history.

Sebastian as papery, waifs of flailing speech, tentative, undecided, gossamer.
The questions, the renderings, the doubting eyes and what they see.

A prison cell in Mali is the same as one in Senegal, Guinea and Burkina Faso.
The small square window, the hole in the ground, the rice and sauce.

We are the architects of our own failed relations; we are our own harbingers.
Their first presence a glint in the dark, to rivet, crisp error as wintry.

Of ways woven in dreams, of every interest along with every bluing fear; no more flinching against the still breath of the sniper, its erasure.

Where was the whispering? Its retracing of steps, or more creatures of habit?
What of our peacetime assumptions, as conditioned, ashen, weary?

You think hot chocolate, and I drink it. You crack the marzipan, its halves into two tiffin bowls; we dip unleavened bread into the thin soup.

A gesture like the frangipani thrust into a rifle, large petals like wings afloat.
In the river beyond Salzburg, before Chopin's berceuse went blue.

Within these concrete walls, three Bambara initiate themselves, the last year of a seven-year cycle, the chiwara mask made of straw and large twigs.

Between his waltz and nocturne, your smile at your grandfather's Latin; your loud laugh, the men helpless, serenading into bunker walls.

As thick a handguard forward, as God-given an inner strength to say no.
To walk back to the ramparts a poet, with the promise of a ballad.

No good could come out of this is Rilke's refrain, and quivering thought.
Of wishes, of a life less forbidding, less foreboding, more luminous.

A prison cell in Mali is the same as one in Gambia, Ghana and Cape Verde.
The lack of daylight, the shuffling feet, the mound of hessian sacks.

How to take one more step into the unknown, when one already knows?
The eventuality of such things, worlds beyond Ludwig, his firm gaze?

Into the shifting point of aim, one more grasp of Innsbruck at sundown?
Its deep curves, and warm smells, Mendelssohn from the sidewalk.

The crackle does not sound, no cradlesong against tympanum; it is nearing
as marked as bigness to this room, your chambered round a memory.

In the note is a votive moment, tenuous offering, its sigh like a paper nautilus.
Carrier pushed away from the bolt, Wittgenstein's aphorism in hand.

That is the sound of an eternal sorry, as the nyama prays to the morning light.
He draws a lizard on the left wall. To keep out the bad, to keep us safe.

# FACELESS FLOWERS

## Katelin Farnsworth

I thought when I left
that everything would change.
The music would change. The flowers would grow taller.
They would grow faces.
The sun would beat down harder.

Over breakfast I opened the paper, nearly spilt the milk;
your face plastered all over the black and white

How funny to suggest that I miss the old days; the days
where we were trapped like spiders in jars,
curling around the corners uselessly.
And now your dog-worn face is back there, in the smoky blue
haze, scattered with hardship, regret, redemption.
I remember the matron peeling us to pieces, mixing her
words with our wounds; floating through the halls.

One of these days I think I'm going to go outside
and carve your face into the brick, try
and reimagine the way our hearts pressed into one another,
thumping against each other; feelings rubbing, battling the days,
the sun streaming in, the sky cracking, my words falling like silk.
I have nowhere to be, no one to see now that I've been set free.
But I know this
freedom is just another kind of prison, suffocating me all over
again.

Remember when we used to cling to one another, hands locked
together through the fence?

My hands shaking in the cold, how could you, how could you

and now,

you're dying in there; I'm dying out here,

and the flowers, that never really looked like people and don't have the faces I thought they'd have,

are dying too.

## BONFIRE ASHES

**Margaret Wilmot**

What happens inside their brains?
These people who read
*The Book of Great Dictators* for
gardening tips:

How to slash and burn
the nettles of now. Prune the past more delicately –
that is, if you wish to keep
a bed for nostalgia.

Burn all diseased clippings.
What happens inside their brains, these people
who make denial
their drug of choice?

Does the axon terminal
wave excitedly at the synapse edge, while no
chemical ferry arrives for
its impulse?

Are the dendrites damaged?
Perhaps the protein receptors
are distorted, as with nicotine, and, indeed, heroin.
Or is it a question,

yet again, of burning?
Electrics sparking
into flame instead of charging with positive intent
through the neuronal channel –

maybe even setting
fire to the oily inner wall.
*Your CAT scan has revealed a dark hollow of tissue loss,
and – see here? –*

*this curious residue, as of bonfire ashes.*

# AFRICA COME BACK

**Rehan Qayoom**

*After Faiz.*

Come Back, I've heard the surge of your drums
Come Back, my heart beats lasciviously

    'Africa come back'

Come Back, I've raised my face out from the dust
Come Back, I've peeled off the pellicle of sorrow from my eyes
Come Back, I've snatched away my arms from the grip of pain
Come Back, I've wrenched apart the hasp of gloom

    'Africa come back'

The shackle's clasps have made the mace too much to bear
So I've fashioned a mould by ripping the strap round my neck

    'Africa come back'

The bear's death-eyes blaze in every lair
Enemy blood has reddened the negritude of night

    'Africa come back'

The ground is pirouetting with me Africa
Rivers throbbing to the rhythm pouring out of the woods
I am Africa, your stature mirrors mine
I am you; my gait is the gait of your lions

'Africa come back'

Come stride like your lions
'Africa come back'


*A Dirge after the slogan of the African socialist democrats.*

*Faiz Ahmed Faiz.* Nuskhaha e Wafa. *(Karwan, 1984). 278).*

# ANTSCAPE, HUNGARY

**Sheila Hamilton**

They just couldn't keep away
from the tatty building,
a building which must have known in its time
many ants, their processions and surges,
their coming in and their going out.

Northern wood ant,
yellow meadow ant,
black garden ant,
blood-red slavemaker ant,
all of these,

and in they marched, in huge numbers,
some in rainy weather,
others when the streets were hot,
some arriving at night, some preferring the daytime,
all of them pushed onward by ant-logic, formic desires.

The cleaner brandished ant-powder,
the label showing an ant big as a mouse,
an ambitious ant, a grandiose ant
but the problem wasn't size, it was numbers,
that ant had friends and friends and friends and friends

# VANISHING TRICK

## Pat Borthwick

Bouquets of roses, a white rabbit, doves –
your hands are expert at hiding these.

They can swallow whole packs of cards, an egg,
silk scarves. Me. Your sequined sleeves

shine in the spotlight. Look! Now you see it,
now often you don't. Through a puff of glitter,

here come your fists with knuckles
as white and hard as marble (no illusion),

each thumb locking your fingers down. But
now we're back home and on our own stage,

*Down, down,* they insist one after the other.
They can, in the sleight of a blink,

raise colours on my arms and around my eyes.
How did I reach the bottom of the stairs

–and so fast? *Show me a different trick,* I whisper,
hoping this time you'll conjure up love

but you open your hands full of wasps, cup
my face. *I'm sorry,* you say, *it won't happen again.*

# SEEING THE SUN

**Brigid Murray**

My carer comes early. She
opens the curtains at exactly
that moment when sky
and streetlights are equally dim
and the window shows a glimpse
of roofs laid pale with frost.

Tyre treads on waking
roads sound like Velcro
ripping while cars cough
and hesitate before edging
in to join the queue
for the motorway.

She balances a bowl of water
on my belly. I make no attempt
to reach it but lie, holding it steady
with my breath

as a tiny reflection of another
reflection of sky
refracts in a corner
of a mirror far away, up high:

showing the smoothed and rounded
edges of long-held truths scraped
back to their original apostasies;
the inconvenient fractals at their heart.

# HAND-FOOT COORDINATES

**Brigid Murray**

Last October I searched the beach for you
and found an empty shell,
pink and plump as a child's toe. And before that,

in the bonus days of June, you rested
your feet on my knees
and I stroked
each foot towards me, my hands joined
over the smooth arch, my thumbs
praying along your sole, plaiting
and unplaiting my fingers
through your swollen toes: on, over,
through and under, meditatively
moving the tideless oedema; plaiting
love with death.

It ended in August.

Now, it's October again,
and still my dreaming mind cradles
each foot in empty, waking air.

# BEGINNING

**Kate Harmond Allen**

Harsh.
Three dark days and two black nights,
unbirth'd, she laboured
hard.

Howl.
Hailstones hammer casements,
mocking her agony with rattles and drums.
Freakish storms
stop up the earth's renewal,
seal sap in bud and branch,
frost fields with hard hoar.
Foul.

May -
that bright, brave bloom plucked
by force, flipped, flayed, flattened,
stripped and splayed and split asunder,
left limp in a flint-lined ditch.
Pray.

Frail,
she slips. She sighs her last.
A rip, a rush, a scarlet gush –
a flood, a force.
A fist.
I flicker, fold, and flex.
I gasp and gape.
Wail.

# DWELLING PLACE

**Miriam Patrick**

*Matthew 8:20*
That summer, the city grew too risky.
Moved along so many times we had no rest
and when they finally let us be, the late night
party-goers travelling home, would harass us
from malice or stupidity. And so we left,
camped on the waste ground out beyond
the station, a place where tracks gave up
the ghost, halting in a wilderness of tired
buddleia and willow herb, gravel underfoot,
where once or twice we saw a lizard dart
beneath the shadowed wing print of a hawk.
At night we often woke dry-mouthed,
hearing the foxes bark, a shout like pain.
They came and went quite fearlessly,
their home the disused tunnel's gaping mouth.

The sun was punishing, the corrugated iron
and plastic sheets we used to build our hide
bounced back its rays to space. At night
it creaked and grumbled as it slowly cooled.
Above us on a ledge, a seagull hugged
its makeshift nest, laughed defiance
as the trains passed by. Out of view, we saw
the lines of weary faces turned our way
as, unaware of anything beyond the track,
they travelled on. At night long lines
of goods trains squealed and clanked
off on their journeys north, we counted them
like sheep before we finally slept and woke
at dawn still tired and craving rest;
envied the fox its lair, the gull its nest.

## KELP STALK

**Pat Bowen**

on the beach remembers
a fluid kind of entanglement
that lingers in this desiccated form.

A jackdaw pushes it aside,
wants something much more succulent.

In such a situation who would not impersonate a dragon?

See the curved and split reptilian tongue,
scales along a sinuous spine,
this impressive head raised, ready to roar.

## TAKING THE WEIGHT

**Pat Bowen**

Leather, oak, steel
meet in us: take your seat.
Feel our struts and uprights.

You carried us through city streets.
Did you wonder where we were
before that tatty stall?

You'll never know.
Style and function are what matters
in the business of chairs.

You might devise a story.
Even one well made, like us
will never match

the teeming forest, seam of ore in rock,
tanned skin of beast, and all the work.
Think of that.

# TILL THE PUFFLING COMES

**Christopher Luck**

A head which so devotes itself to beak
that eye and sinew, muscle and cheek
strain toward this orange-slashed Roman nose,
segmented blue and red and yellow flashed.
Such is this horn bearer, this aerial
pocket rhino, this auk with the nasal
promise of the love sonnets of Cyrano.*

Yet puffins are not just beaks - of the genus
*fratercula*, 'little brothers' in monastic black and white,
they turn to pelagic ways when breeding ends
and pigment drains to a dull underbill
that won't see land till summer's colours return,
and nest side fidelity reasserts its pull
on mutual brood patches pulsing
blood-warm round a lilac tinged egg ...
till the puffling comes.

In diving sprees sand eel and herring are
hinged whole by those capacious beaks
for lone chicks who will fledge at night
to stay five years silently at sea,
before procreation in vocal colony
beckons them to cliff top island meets.

But beware the peril of some summer lands,
low flying puffins, for you can be fished from
the sky by Icelanders bearing large nets,
who will rip out your hearts and eat them raw fresh.

So - with your whirring small wings that morph
into furiously paddling fins –
is your long lived silence at sea
a wariness of such danger sensed?

And do you wonder perhaps what might become of that totem
beak when finally it parts
from your puffin heartbeat?

*A fictionalised version of a 17$^{th}$ century French nobleman serving as a soldier (Cyrano de Bergerac), who was a talented swordsman, musician and poet. However, self-doubts because of his very large nose prevented him from expressing his love for his beautiful and distant cousin, Roxanne, except via poems composed on behalf of another officer, for whom she had declared her love, and who had no talent for such things.

# THE GARDEN

## Alex Hamilton-Brown

*"Where Have All The Flowers Gone? "*
*Pete Seeger*

Today, when I turned on the news,
they were listing the flowers of war;
flowers who fell in a foreign land,
re-planted back home in their native soil.

When I turned to my garden,
the news was much better.
No armies of lilies were marching
to slaughter the rose.
No hostile lobelia
were planning a siege on the phlox.
No beautiful despot of garden oppression
was sanctioning torture and pain.

And I thought of a time
when we colourful hominids -
pink and yellow and shades of brown -
measured their lives by gifts
from a plentiful garden
and passions from the skies; but now...
numbers explode like popping seeds
and root where billions already grow.

Now the garden is thinner,
and those who have, survive.
They watch the undernourished starve -
their own roots wither.
And still, with exponential speed

our hominid species' spread,
and this, with growing greed for *more*,
is *less* good for the garden,
and, for those to come.

# GORDON'S

## Charlotte Gann

The sweating ceiling leans in
to hear all the filth we're talking -
contorted wax gargoyles speaking for us.
Our St Vitus fingers dance,
hollowing out mouths, jaws,
grind butts into an evening's ashtray
searching for gold dust.
*He loves me, he loves me not.*
My companion commiserates -
as she always does,
Italian hair weighted by candlelight.
Her life carries other travails.

Come midnight, we'll both turn into
pumpkins, rats, scamper out
into Villiers Street. Or so I think.

In fact we're princesses,
flitting out from under a shadowed door,
seeking lives.

## ALTITUDES OF MEETING AND PARTING

E.E.Nobbs

The Commander sings
"Space Oddity" from the Space Station
before he returns
        to blue Earth.

When we dismantle
the grey steel locker in the basement
I'll find the bullet
        in a crack.

With the right wrenches
they could've fixed it but the plumber
over-torqued the nut —
        now she's stuck.

Watch them
repair ammonia leaks up there
wearing walrus gloves.
        Do you miss

me Major
Tom? The aspen leaves are exploding
like baby spiders
        in this rain.

# FLOOD

**Denise McSheehy**

The garden solid with water, grass only just
holding it. A grey and yellow sky;
sodden air. As if we'd learned how to breathe
in another more fluid dimension
holed up for so long, listening.
This was the best of the light, it wouldn't
get any brighter, rain an organism
fine and persistent fretting at our skins.
Momentarily we saw the sun
before it sunk in murk, the rain
growing heavier, louder, the sound
taking over, mazing our heads. We turned
back, knowing nothing was different
out there where water drained off
the hills, burst from sewers into houses.
And we gathered in an upstairs room
watched the grass gag on wet
the yellow in the sky, once
hopeful, dunked.

# ADDICTED

**Denise McSheehy**

The early dark
when there's still a pallor in the sky;

addictive to stand
looking down

the river oiling its way
south, a stealthy

brimming of the grasses
the river

tonguing the grasses, wetly.
Now it's night - only

the black oily water
shifting very slowly, the tide

drawing it, as if
with a frequency I can't hear;

bits of leaf shimmy
and spin, flare -

I stare at the black water
sense the dip of invisible branches.

# SATURDAY BLUES

## Oz Hardwick

Kenny's in the cafe. *She's been too long,*
he thinks, *what's she doing in there?*
The parking must have nearly run out
and he can see a warden on the far side
of the square. Not doing much at the moment,
though, just staring vacantly down the street.
*She's been too long.*

          The warden's on the corner.
It's not his usual beat, but there's people
off at the moment, so things are stretched.
*I need a bloody holiday*, he thinks,
then suddenly notices his wife, who he thought
was at home, rush across the road further down
and into the expensive lingerie shop.
*What's she doing in there?*

          His wife
rushes into the shop and stops. She's
in a hurry, but wants just the right thing.
It's never simple. *I need a holiday,*
she thinks, feeling the delicate burr
of expensive white lace between
her carefully manicured fingers. Glancing
up, she catches the condescending eye
of the young girl behind the counter.
*What's she looking at?*

          The young girl
stares into space. The money's ok
but she'd rather do something else with her Saturdays.

It's boring. The shop's been open nearly
two hours, and no-one's actually
bought anything yet. She looks
through the window at a woman gazing in.
*What's she looking at? Way too old
for this sort of thing.*

    The woman pauses
by the window. She doesn't really want
anything, doesn't really even see
anything, just wants to take a minute
to gather her composure. She's too clever
to show it, but her heart's racing. As always.
*Way too old for this sort of thing,*
subtly adjusting the bright fabric
secreted beneath her nondescript coat.
*Ah, well. Kenny will be waiting.*

# THE GIFT

## Oz Hardwick

We met on a bridge in the shade of tall buildings.
I recall no details but his neat black suit
and discreet manner, like a high-class waiter,
a faint smell of soap and wet towels.

He passed me a small, scuffed attache case,
spoke a few words in Italian that I didn't understand,
as we walked, shoulder to shoulder, awkward strangers,
before he vanished into an anonymous side-street.

As I headed to the hotel, I noticed cracks in the pavement,
though all around the water continued to rise.
I climbed the stairs to my room, left the lights
turned off, rested the case on the bed.

Inside was a small garden, with bonsai trees,
a mirror lake, manicured grass. Birds
swooped low, skittered at their reflections.
I bent my head low, listened to their songs.

# THE MANDOLIN LESSON

## Oz Hardwick

Out of breath, he begins with something easy,
pull notes like stones from beaches or histories from shelves,
asking the obvious questions: *What am I saying?*
*Where am I going?*

            The floor is painted with seaweed,
branching like lungs as windows gasp for air.
His wrist flexes, stiff railway points
shifting tracks, arriving slightly late.
His fingers are necks of French aristocrats,
bending to the blade.

            Open pages flutter
to here and now, concentrating on three chords,
a simple index for freed fingers, loosening,
swimming between stacks of books from which crabs scuttle.

Easy, easy: a slow, simple soundtrack
for shipwrecked libraries and tales of the sea.

# PATCHWORK LANGUAGE

**Roger Elkin**

You've amassed this stash of material –
scraps, samples, hand-me-downs –
colourful stuff you just have to possess,
make your own, hoard for future use;
though, never knowing their wealth's extent,
are reduced to trusting their potential as they
push themselves to be re-used.

Their first trick's the best: letting you
think you're in control as you arrange what
you've imagined as fit for purpose -
say, a range of shades in subtleties of tone,
balancing dark against light, and suited to
the backing and padding underpinning the scheme,
for, after all, what lies behind and in-between
adds meanings to the surface reading.

Next, they offer you the option of following
a traditional pattern, drafting it out on paper,
framing block after block, but taking care
your material's not skewed and stretched
against the grain;
          or, since you class yourself
master of your craft, you're allowed to interpret it
at will, filling in the shape, picking out the rhythm,
and stitching-through the visual imagery
in keeping with your theme.

                    Either way,
they know you'll need to allocate yourself
some latitude to accommodate all the skill,

imagination and time that's been invested -

    for that, a wiggly line can be most forgiving –

though, take note:
too much attention spent plotting metres into feet,
or using material that's skimpy –

    filigree and gossamer scrunch puckering up –

might just frustrate your grand designs,
even blow a poem's cover.

## WEB WEAVER
*After the wire sculpture by Helen Walsh*

### Gabriel Griffin

She'd always lied. Her perfidy
shone sugar-coated, the sticky threads
of sweet-tongued fabrication
hardening to steel. She span a web
of falsehood where our words
stuck and swung while, mesmerized,
we watched her dance down the trembling lines -
then pounce.

We vowed revenge, we'd "get 'er"! But as from
a craftwork lampshade - string, glue, balloon - the
escapes through windows in the net, she slipped
out of the tangled web she'd spun. She left
only the outline of the self
we thought we'd known. We searched
but when the sun slashed through
the frame of lies we found
just random shades upon the grass, runes
that none of us can understand.

# NICHE

## Mark Totterdell

An Easter walk. The spring delayed, the lanes
all lined with leafless hedges, villages
unpeopled. You seek out church after church,
enter each porch, stand poised before each door
of dark and ancient wood that will not give.
You turn around. Each outer arch points up
towards a statueless and shallow niche,
none quite the same, though every one contains
its cup of roughcast clay, empty for now,
and barely firm enough, you fear, to hold
your eggshell faith in the returning sun.

# I REMEMBER LEAVING

**Valerie Bridge**

I remember leaving the queue in the playground
*schtumm,* my sister wanting the cod liver oil and malt
on the spoon they didn't wash between each dosing
and the chalked hopscotch squares.

I remember leaving that queue in the playground,
the smell of fish oil like glue, the lip-smacking
of my sister licking my untasted spoon,
her ribboned pigtails bobbing. Up close

I remember leaving the queue of kids
longing for a lick, the outstretched spoons,
the teacher's face screwed up with hoping
to be done with kids hopping around.

I remember leaving the queue, *schtumm,*
going through the 'girls only' entrance,
hugging a cardboard box of chalks
swapped for a ballerina jewellery box.

I remember leaving the queue, running
over asphalt ground, up to the headmistress'
glass cage office, where she sat poker faced,
and her ruler tapped out safe time.

I remember leaving the English school, behind
the railway yard, the shunt of engines,
whistle of steam, smell of wet coal,
the bridge over nowhere to be found.

I remember leaving that safe as houses
school, getting home to my mother's
red face over my fingers clutching chalks,
the way she spat out, *'you hev go back get it,*

how she hit at me with her ruler,
and I was *'schtumm'*, measuring
the long trek. I remember leaving
my mother's face behind.

## ACTING MY AGE

**Camilla Lambert**

When I was sixteen I wore straight skirts,
cardigans, blouses sewed by my aunt
from Butterick patterns pinned, folded
into their packets to use another time.
Anyone would have thought me thirty five.

When I was thirty five I danced round
a birthday bonfire, fingers touched flame,
the stars crackled in discordant languages
wind in my hair tempted with anything,
everything. I could have been twenty three.

When I was twenty three all I wanted
was a kindly man to bring me tea in bed,
pay the mortgage on the dot, cherry trees
frothing down the garden path each spring.
I talked of pensions as if I were forty eight.

When I was forty eight I began to see
my eyes had become my mother's, a droop
of disappointment in the corner, flickering
with anxiety when checking for the exit.
My soul belonged to a woman of sixty nine.

When I was sixty nine the dawn came earlier;
released from work's dreariness I woke
to blackbirds pouring out fresh promises.
Age brought surprises, once-bolted doors
opened into snaking alleyways: I was twelve again.

When I was twelve I knew how death tasted,
cold as a pebble in a mountain stream,
and what lay behind the warning 'Beware
the wash of passing ships'. Staggering
up the shifting beach I had reached fifty six.

When I was fifty six I took a younger lover,
sex coloured my life crimson, purple, gold,
around me a cloud of flickering butterflies,
each day another day in paradise, bright
as if I was in love and only sixteen.

# FROU-FROU AT THE PANORAMA

## Camilla Lambert

Fingers aching, she piles the plates,
arranges tomato, onion, cucumber, cheese:
another day without his face
swimming up from the lunchtime hordes.

Only once had he returned since their glory time;
she still dared not speak his name
though from the start she had known who he was.
His face half in shade, he had laughed like he used to
as she said *Frou-frou. Remember?*

Each year the filigree creases of her skin
grow more like the bark of the twisted olives
that grip the slope below the taverna,
contorted trunks giving shelter to lizards and snakes.

She resists the thought his god's gaze has gone wider,
balks at knowing he'll not come back
to this view of misted hills, listen
to the evening bell hung by the white-washed church,
never again greet her *Frou-frou? Remember?*

As visitors stream from the coaches she stays keen-eyed,
a falcon alert to movement, filtering false alarms;
her blood is still red like the poppies
and the stab of his absence is as sharp as prickly acanthus,

until at last the blisters of bark thicken, close together,
the whorls and the knots conquer her fingers.
In the end there is no answer but a flurry of leaves
silver-green in the moonlight
when anyone asks *Frou-frou– remember?*

# PERSPECTIVE

## Chris McLaughlin

From the sky, the things we've built
look like circuit boards. Not at all lovely
like the greens and yellows of the fields.
I can see the interconnectivity of life.
How a canal stretches out towards the sea.

How a boat looks so tiny in the vast
blue; its jet stream stretching behind like
a slug trail. I am on a long haul flight that
never ends. The attendants are attractive
and the food cart is well stocked; there is

a steady stream of beer and yet all I can do
is whine. I'm sorry. I have forgotten my
destination. A long legged blonde brings
me another drink. Asks me not to think
too loud. *You're scaring the other passengers.*

## FIVE POETS TAKE A WALK IN THE COUNTRY

**Tony Watts**

    ...in search of the Muse, who naturally
went into hiding (her favourite game, after all).

Today she's playing squirrels -
somewhere out here,
in this fold of the Blackdown Hills,
she has hidden the nut
that contains the seed
of a poem.

We descend from the car park to the lake. Could it be there,
in the root-dark of that rhododendron island
where no-one goes? No-one has ever been?

We linger at the bridge
in a wistful silence...
                      (Everyone wants to be water

    - not the headlong river that bruises itself on rocks
    in its haste to escape the source, still less the sea,
    tossing and sighing at the end of the moon's leash -

    not these, but *lakewater* - water that has come home,
    that fills its space completely, that presents
    an untroubled surface over settled depths.)

Reluctantly we move away
and take the narrow path into the woods
(Is that the rain-rinsed song of a bird
in the high trees - or the Muse's mocking laughter?)
Maybe she's hidden it here, where the beech-boles raise
their smoky torsos in an ancient dance.

*

The lower lake is shedding a skin -
it slithers like silk down a stone staircase
and disappears among billows of water dropwort
- perhaps it's there

...or there, where a solitary orchid burns -
a candle in the grass (may it soon
get a bee in its bonnet and seed a conflagration.)

*

Should we ask the bearded fisherman on the bridge?
Or the lady whose dog,
slicing the lake like an otter,
smashes its stick in an excess of eagerness?

*

The sky darkens and a shabby rain
shepherds us into a pub. Could it be here?
*A pint of Exmoor Gold and a sonnet please.*
We dry out over a meal (how easily
the body is appeased, while the spirit still hungers.)

*

And now the final lap (along lanes to avoid
the sodden grasses). Subtle shifts of scenery in the sky
reveal the backdrop in a glimpse of blue.

A frieze of bovine faces,
like trophies hung along the hedge-top, and beyond them
a late sun settles on a row of oaks
as though it were a homecoming.

                                                  Is it there,
in that golden wood at the far end of a field?

"There is much to appreciate in Nduka's joyous language, his percussive rhythms; his sense of movement runs like a river..."
    -**Library Journal**

"In *Nine East,* Nduka locates the grace of our graphic, bodied days, in verse somehow both free and arresting – volleyed between playful compound neologisms and stark, unaffected prose these lines capture the poet's life in all its quotidian wonder, the word recalling always our dual anatomies, formed of cell and sentence. The edges blur as we enter the pace of these pages, knowing ourselves here, asking ourselves (as Nduka asks himself, and us) why we are *waiting for a bus as the poem's face is lifting off, almost slipping out of the page, making room for the unintended*. They are poems for now, and for here."
    - **Lynne DeSilva-Johnson,**
        Managing Editor *Exit Strata*

Available at
www.amazon.com / www.amazon.co.uk
www.barnesandnoble.com / www.spmpublications.com

# THE CURE

**Robin Lindsay Wilson**

Just when her mother needed grandchildren
and her aggressive cousins were trading up,
she sagged at the same time as the cushions
on a blank afternoon surrounded by choices.

Her kitchen knife only cut vegetable slime,
chopped, wormy stems and shrivelled seeds
to make a meal from a hard-faced garden.
When she sniffed the garlic on her thumb
the bulb burst into spores of sneezing rot.
But her black eyes lifted and stayed proud,
in every steely direction except the mirror.

The circle on her father's kitchen calendar
marked an uncertain promise to celebrate
but the new year sun came up too soon,
or it refused to kindle in the east that year –
either way she failed to signal generosity.
His soup cooled and her father was gone.

She settled in the deep greasy settee folds.
Her head attracted blue skies and lovebirds.
She auditioned wines for their forgetfulness,
pretending each daydream was a gateway.
After that she bought a steel potato-peeler
and shaved off her threatening imagination.

# THE GREEN POST

**Lydia Suarez**

We have been left
to drink mud and pose for x rays,
toil at jobs of monotony and deadlines
at an age where we fall asleep in armchairs.

Do you remember how it rained the first time
or are your memories odorless and sterile

I was a girl easily impressed by
Rimbaud and Turkish coffee
You wrote uninspired papers
and spoke of embassy parties.

Do you remember bare arms and a rocky path,
owls and spiders
a serpent that swallowed us whole
only flicking matches after they burned your finger.

Now I find you among paint cans and Christmas lights
lost in your garage
beside a house with a wide screen and a waffle maker
your face immobile with age and indifference.

Do you remember a balcony with the faint smell of seaweed,
 kissing as we leaned against a green post.
or are the tips of your finger
no longer a faded yellow.

## MEMENTO MORI

**Jenny Donnison**

The pine table is scrubbed and ready.
Trace knots and splits, old softwood wounds.

A vase off-centre, filled anyhow with flowers:
frill-petal tulips, lilies thick as tongues.

Place dull-eyed fish on a crackle-glazed plate;
grey-green mackerel stippled black.

Bottles of wine, a bowl of pomegranates.
Pulp-soft oysters on ragged shells.

That second-hand book you will not read.
Your overcoat, the scarf with skulls.

Your guitar, old flyers, photographs.
A half-smoked pack trails threads of gold.

The list you wrote, your wrist watch.
A candle lit against the dark.

# SPINNING TIME

**Ann Hamlett**

I lost a poem in the night
perfectly placed on pristine page,
stanza after stanza
filled the bold white space.

> *'Buds on trees stretch out*
> *tiny hands to feel the air,*
> *catch silver raindrops.'*

I lost a poem in the night;
thought I could remember it.
In my dream I read it out
over and over - every bit.

> *'Almond blossoms peep.*
> *Catkins fluff yellow dusters*
> *comb air with sweetness.'*

I lost a poem in the night
hoped if I held the strap line ...
repeat and repeat in my mind
I'd unfurl it like a flag by morning.

> *'Stately foxgloves climb*
> *over tumbled garden walls;*
> *bees buzz in bonnets.'*

I lost a poem in the night
and I lost you too. Only in dreams
do you return to me,
to slip away like dawn dew.

                                    *'Sepia tinted...*
                              *a grey damp mist hangs over*
                                *beleaguered landscape.'*

I lost a poem in the night.
                                        *'Wind whorls static air"*

In my dreams...
                                *'weaves silk sheen gossamer threads.'*

shrouded mists shimmer...
                                              *'Nine maidens spin time'*
*'Spin time...*
              *Spin time...'*
                                                    through the night.

## YOU SHOULD GO ...

**Anne Hamlett**

You know the Magnolia tree,
the one in bloom with large cup-cake
pink petals that glow like sun
through rose quartz. Well,
nearby there's an old cricked gate
with rough wormed wood.

It's there, just there where
the hidden path winds up the hill
covered with neck-high meadowsweet
in summer, with their frothy cream
heads and delicate scent of almonds,
oh... and mind the nettles; they thrive
in the hollowed-out shade beneath
the stand of oak. You must pass
under lichen cloaked branches,
careful with the one which toppled
last winter under weight of snow...

it's not far to go now.
Soon as you round the bend you'll see
a spread of water that glows in green
stippled sunlight. If you're quiet
as you head for the clump of reeds
and don't disturb the moorhens,
or the corncrakes with their 'krek- krek'
calls, you'll find a mound of moss
hidden below weeping willows;
well that's it.

Lie there in evening light
and you might see an otter
as it fishes in sliver ringed ripples,
until the crescent moon tiptoes
across a starry sky - it's there,

just there, where all
is as it should be.
                You'll see.
                          You should go.

# THE EXPLODING HORSE, 1922

## Mary Oliver

*Can you see that couple?*

Yes I can.

*What are they doing?*

You can see perfectly well what they are doing.

*In a field of clover?*

It's as good a place as any.

*Who are they?*

He's an itinerant farm-worker. A stowaway. Came in on the last freighter.

*Look at his back muscles!*

Yes. He's proud of his physique.

*And her?*

That's Myrtle, the farmer's daughter

*Oh, she's so plump and gorgeous!*

Yes, she is.

*So where's the farmer?*

He's in town. It's market day. He won't be back till tomorrow.

*Can I hear them laughing?*

Yes, you can. Both have had tough lives up till now. This is their moment.

*I can see that!*

Unfortunately, in their haste, they have left the gate open.

**BANG!**

*What was that? Sounded like a gun going off.*

It was Stanley, the cart-horse. He has exploded.

*What? A horse can explode?*

Yes. If it gets into a field of fresh clover it will eat and eat until its belly fills up with methane gas and it explodes.

*Huh? Is that what happened?*

Yes. I told you they left the gate open.

*The stink's awful.*

What do you expect?

*And listen to their language!*

Yes. It is colourful.

*What's the farmer going to do when he gets back?*

Kill the pair of them if he gets the chance. He's a violent man.

*So what'll they do?*

They will burn the carcass and bury the remains.

*How are they going to explain Stanley's disappearance to the farmer?*

They are going to leave a note on the kitchen table:
'Horse thieves broke in and stole Stanley.
We're out searching for him. Supper's in the oven'.

*So do you think they're going to run away together?*

Yes, I do.

*Will they live happily ever after?*

No, they won't. But it's an original beginning.

## GIRL IN BATH STREET

A.C. Clarke

She's dressed like streetwalkers I've seen
leaning over Kings Cross cars,
the hottest of pants,
swish of blonded mane, white legs stretching
down, down to end at last
in heels awkward as stilts.
*Asking for it.*

She doesn't seem to be asking
for anything. Any game she's on
looks serious. No lipstick.
She's staring at her iPhone
but, yes, she's walking the street,
passes twice in her tottery stride.

All the stock responses
knot under my ribs:
sour, old woman's envy,
pity, that *droit de dame*
of lady bountifuls . What I really feel
is fear. A beautiful,

breakable thing lies open
to the clumsiest touch.
Above us both the sky
glows orange. Whatever the stars
are up to we can't see it,
only the reflection
of all our burning lives.

# WILD PETER

## A.C.Clarke

        i

His name was given him,
as a new name is given to a bought dog, engraved

on the collar they made him wear
after he went missing. He learned it
as a dog learns to come to the master's call.

His name was one of two things he could say.
The other was 'King George'.

        ii

He was wild because he was found in a forest
He was wild because he made a humming noise
He was wild because he had shocking table manners

He was wild because he would not sleep in a bed
He was wild because he was good at climbing trees
He was wild because his nails needed clipping

He was wild because he kept his hat on
He was wild because he liked sucking twigs
He was wild because he was charmed by a watch

He was wild because he would not dance to the fiddle
He was wild because he did not powder his hair
He was wild because he mourned his master like a dog.

        ii

And they painted his portrait
And they raised his headstone
And his grave is still visited by flowers.

*Introducing*

# TravelTime Shorts

TravelTime Shorts is a new imprint of Sentinel Writing and Publishing Company which will publish a single short story up to 5000 words, or a short poetry collection up to 300 lines long. The 300 lines may be a single poem or a collection of two or more shorter poems.

TravelTime Shorts publishes electronically only.

To learn more, request an information pack by email from traveltimeshorts@gmail.com

# EVENING CAME AND MORNING CAME

## Maria Bennett

> *God called the light 'day', and darkness he called 'night'.*
> *Evening came and morning came: the first day.*
>                               Gen 1:5

When they first met in a Dublin gallery
the courtyard was lit white, acolytes
swept along, candles raised.
Evening came.

> The curtains were turquoise, drawn tight
> in a strange house where they told stories
> and he sang and picked a tune;
>   and morning came, the first day.

*We tell each other more than we tell anyone,*
he sang in a roof garden in June. Evening
came.

> In Donegal, there was a continental kiss in a hotel.
> *We are so wrong,* she said,
> *that we are right,* he added,
> and morning came.

*I am your shadow,* she said.
*Or are you mine?*
Hard light hurt; she needed
evening.
Morning came.

\*

She stares into his face as rain rages,
and holds his hands to unfold memories,
to hear his lyrics and melodies,
to rescue days rinsed away in streams.

His warm hands still squeeze life into hers
and she always finishes his lines by heart,
*Soon the dove will come with an olive branch,*
she says. *We will be home and wet,* he sings.

Evening comes and morning comes,
the fifteen hundred and seventeenth day.

# ENDURANCE

**Mantz Yorke**

Nothing but suffering, being slowly crushed
all these months in the screaming dark,
oak ribs groaning, bowing to the thickening ice,
and coldness trickling through sprung seams.

Ahead and astern leaden leads long ago yielded
hope to certainty. All I have is within
an upturned lifeboat on the ice: the ship is left
as it always was, a veneer on empty air.

Suddenly a splitting of timbers, a settling
lower amid the pack: not long now
till the dead weight of iron drags downward
and the pack's teeth crunchingly close.

And so my flimsy boat, life's refuge
against the spearing bitterness,
must be righted if I am to face
the hissing vicissitudes of the sea.

> *Why haul an open boat*
> *towards a sea so cold*
> *it will suck your life in minutes,*
> *whose wind-split spray*
> *will flense skin from flesh,*
> *flesh from bone, body from soul?*
>
> *Why not slip away,*
> *letting numbness spread inward*
> *from the blackening extremities*
> *of being, and warm you*
> *like a winter horizon's*
> *crimson sun ?*

You tempt me, Southern Cross, with your invitation
yet, like that other at my side, you are a figment –
stars in accidental conjunction
and your heart the infinite void.

I shall put thee behind me,
strike northward, and not look back.

www.ingramcontent.com/pod-product-compliance
Lightning Source LLC
Chambersburg PA
CBHW031457040426
42444CB00007B/1129